Washington MYSTICS

by Charlie Beattie

Copyright © 2026 by Press Room Editions. All rights reserved. No part of this book may be used or reproduced in any manner whatsoever, including internet usage, without written permission from the copyright owner, except in the case of brief quotations embodied in critical articles and reviews.

Book design by Kate Liestman
Cover design by Kate Liestman

Photographs ©: Ric Tapia/AP Images, cover; Bruce Bennett/Getty Images Sport/Getty Images, 4, 7, 9; Otto Greule Jr./Allsport/Getty Images Sport/Getty Images, 10; Doug Pensinger/Allsport/Getty Images Sport/Getty Images, 13, 14; Jim Bryant/AP Images, 16; Nick Wass/AP Images, 19; Leon Bennett/Getty Images Sport/Getty Images, 20, 22; G. Fiume/Getty Images Sport/Getty Images, 25; Chris Coduto/Getty Images Sport/Getty Images, 27; Scott Taetsch/Getty Images Sport/Getty Images, 29

Press Box Books, an imprint of Press Room Editions.

ISBN
979-8-89469-020-9 (library bound)
979-8-89469-033-9 (paperback)
979-8-89469-058-2 (epub)
979-8-89469-046-9 (hosted ebook)

Library of Congress Control Number: 2025931642

Distributed by North Star Editions, Inc.
2297 Waters Drive
Mendota Heights, MN 55120
www.northstareditions.com

Printed in the United States of America
082025

ABOUT THE AUTHOR

Charlie Beattie is a writer, editor, and former sportscaster. Originally from Saint Paul, Minnesota, he now lives in Charleston, South Carolina, with his wife and son.

TABLE OF CONTENTS

CHAPTER 1
THRILLING FINALE   5

CHAPTER 2
CAPITAL BEGINNINGS   11

CHAPTER 3
MYSTICAL STRUGGLE   17

CHAPTER 4
WINNERS IN WASHINGTON   23

SUPERSTAR PROFILE
ELENA DELLE DONNE   28

QUICK STATS   30
GLOSSARY   31
TO LEARN MORE   32
INDEX   32

CHAPTER 1

THRILLING FINALE

The Washington Mystics needed a bucket. So, they drew up a play for their biggest star. Forward Elena Delle Donne caught a pass with the clock ticking down. She rose up for a jump shot. New York Liberty forward Breanna Stewart stayed with Delle Donne the whole way. Stewart swatted the shot out of bounds.

Elena Delle Donne (11) averaged 16.7 points per game in 2023.

The Mystics were tied with the Liberty 88–88. The two teams were facing off on the final day of the 2023 Women's National Basketball Association (WNBA) season. New York had been one of the league's best teams all year. But Washington had come out firing. The Mystics led by 12 points early in the fourth quarter. However, the Liberty charged back. And with 21 seconds left, Stewart buried a shot to tie the game.

After Stewart's block, only 0.5 seconds remained in the game. That left enough time for Washington to get a shot off. The Mystics had a plan. They designed a play for Brittney Sykes.

Brittney Sykes scored 20 points against the Liberty in the final game of the 2023 season.

Natasha Cloud stood on the baseline. She waited for the play to develop. Delle Donne set a screen for Sykes. Then Sykes ran to the middle of the lane. Cloud lobbed up a pass. Sykes hung in the air and caught the ball. She released her shot in a flash.

The quick shot was right on target. The buzzer sounded just before the ball fell through the basket. Sykes raced up the court celebrating the win. Cloud waved goodbye to the home Liberty fans.

DEFENSE TO OFFENSE

Brittney Sykes entered the WNBA in 2017. She quickly became one of the league's best defenders. In 2023, she made the league's All-Defensive First Team for the second time. But Sykes could also score. She averaged a career-high 15.9 points per game in 2023.

Sykes (left) and Natasha Cloud (right) celebrate beating the Liberty on the final day of the 2023 season.

Washington's win clinched a 19–21 record. That secured a playoff spot. Sykes's shot proved the Mystics could hang with the league's best.

CHAPTER 2

CAPITAL BEGINNINGS

The WNBA started in 1997. After a successful first season, the league expanded. The Washington Mystics were one of two new teams in 1998.

Nikki McCray led the Mystics in their first season. The point guard averaged a team-high 17.7 points per game. In the Mystics' fourth game, they took on

Nikki McCray made the All-Star Game three times while she played with Washington.

the Utah Starzz. McCray had one of her best performances. She scored 29 points and added six assists. McCray helped the Mystics earn their first victory. But wins were rare for the Mystics that season. They finished the year 3–27.

In 1999, the Mystics had the top pick in the WNBA Draft. They picked Chamique Holdsclaw. The forward soon became one of the top stars in the league. In 2000, Holdsclaw lifted the Mystics to the playoffs for the first time. By 2002, she led the league in points and rebounds per game. But Holdsclaw suffered an injury during the season. The Mystics struggled without her. The team went 3–10 in its last 13 games.

Chamique Holdsclaw averaged 18.3 points per game during her six seasons with the Mystics.

    Holdsclaw returned for the 2002 playoffs. In the first round, Washington faced the Charlotte Sting. Holdsclaw racked up 26 points and 13 rebounds

13

Murriel Page spent the first eight seasons of her career with the Mystics.

in Game 1, helping the Mystics earn a win. Game 2 was in Charlotte. Many Mystics fans traveled to the game. After the Mystics won, fans cheered for the players as they left the arena.

The Mystics faced the Liberty in the next round. With eight minutes to go in Game 1, the Mystics trailed by 11 points. Then Washington forward Murriel Page turned it on. She finished the game with 17 points off the bench. Her scoring helped the Mystics win 79–74.

New York bounced back. The Liberty won the next two games and ended Washington's season. But Mystics fans had plenty of hope for the future.

HISTORIC OWNER

Sheila C. Johnson helped create the BET network. The businesswoman became the first Black female billionaire in American history. In 2005, she bought part of the Mystics. While she didn't own all of the team, she began serving as the team's president. That title meant she was fully in charge of the Mystics.

CHAPTER 3

MYSTICAL STRUGGLE

Heading into the 2004 WNBA playoffs, the Mystics were rolling. The team had won five of six games to end the season. And they were winning without Chamique Holdsclaw. The star forward had left the team for personal reasons. So, Alana Beard stepped up. The rookie guard ran Washington's offense. The Mystics opened the

Alana Beard (20) averaged 13.1 points per game during her rookie season.

playoffs against the Connecticut Sun. Beard poured in 13 points and recorded eight rebounds. She led the Mystics to an upset in Game 1.

However, the Mystics fell apart in the next two games. They committed 29 turnovers and lost the series. Playoff disappointments piled up after that. The Mystics lost in the first round in 2006 and 2009.

Before the 2010 season, Beard hurt her ankle. Many analysts expected the Mystics to be the worst team in the league without their star. But other players shined in new roles. Forward Crystal Langhorne led the Mystics in scoring. Point guard Lindsey Harding

Crystal Langhorne averaged a team-high 16.3 points per game for the Mystics in 2010.

dished out assists. Veteran Katie Smith played tight defense. Washington finished with a team-record 22 wins. But once again, the Mystics fell in the first round of the playoffs.

Emma Meesseman made 52 percent of her shots in 2014.

Beard never returned to the team after her injury. In her place, Ivory Latta teamed up with Langhorne. They led Washington back to the playoffs in 2013. But the Mystics failed to win a series that year.

The Mystics continued to find talented players. Forward Emma Meesseman broke out in 2014. A year later, she made her first All-Star Game. Both seasons, she helped the Mystics earn a spot in the playoffs. But she couldn't lift Washington out of the first round.

The team needed to try something different. The Mystics were competitive almost every year. But they lacked a star to bring them to the top.

A FAMILY OF COACHES

The Mystics hired Mike Thibault in 2013. The head coach stayed with the team for 10 seasons. He led the Mystics to the playoffs eight times. Thibault stepped down after the 2022 season. The team's head coaching job stayed in the family, though. Mike's son, Eric, took over.

CHAPTER 4

WINNERS IN WASHINGTON

Elena Delle Donne had dominated with the Chicago Sky. The forward won the league's Most Valuable Player (MVP) Award in 2015. But by 2017, she wanted to be closer to her family in Delaware. So, the Mystics traded for Della Donne.

Delle Donne quickly boosted the Mystics. The team won two playoff

Elena Delle Donne averaged 19.7 points per game in her first season with Washington.

series in 2017. The next year was even better. In 2018, the Mystics reached the WNBA Finals for the first time. But Washington fell short of a title. The Seattle Storm swept the series.

Washington came back stronger in 2019. Delle Donne led the league's best offense. Her scoring earned her MVP honors. And she did it all after breaking her nose early in the season. Then she lifted the Mystics back to the Finals.

Washington faced the Connecticut Sun. The teams split the first four games of the series. That set up a winner-take-all Game 5. Delle Donne was playing through a back injury. But she knew her team needed her.

Delle Donne shoots over a Connecticut defender during Game 5 of the 2019 Finals.

The game was tied with 5:15 left. Delle Donne backed down her defender. The MVP then spun to the baseline. She drilled a fadeaway jumper. The Mystics didn't

25

lose the lead from there. They were finally WNBA champs!

The COVID-19 pandemic struck before the 2020 season. Delle Donne chose to sit out the year. Washington struggled without her. Even when Delle Donne came back, the Mystics couldn't win a playoff series.

Delle Donne decided to take a break from basketball after the 2023 season. Washington began to rebuild around new players. Guard

PLAYOFF EMMA

Emma Meesseman was known as a calm player. But she played with aggression in the 2019 playoffs. Her teammates loved it. They started calling her "Playoff Emma." She averaged 19.3 points and 5.6 rebounds in the playoffs. Meesseman went on to earn Finals MVP honors.

Ariel Atkins (7) made a WNBA All-Defensive Team in each of her first five seasons.

Brittney Sykes played tough defense. So did Ariel Atkins. The Mystics took Aaliyah Edwards in the first round of the 2024 draft. The forward showed promise during her rookie year. Mystics fans hoped this new core could lead the team to another championship.

SUPERSTAR PROFILE

ELENA DELLE DONNE

The Washington Mystics had the fourth pick in the 2013 draft. They wanted to take Elena Delle Donne. But the Chicago Sky selected her with the second pick. So, in 2017, the Mystics jumped at the chance to trade for Delle Donne.

Few players could score as easily as Delle Donne. The sharp-shooting forward kept the Mystics competitive for years. And she led the team to its first championship.

Delle Donne made history in the 2019 season. She drained more than 50 percent of her shots. She also made more than 40 percent of her three-pointers. And she sank more than 90 percent of her free throws. Delle Donne was the first WNBA player to hit all those marks in a season. She joined basketball stars such as Steph Curry and Kevin Durant in the "50-40-90 club."

Delle Donne made the All-Star Game in her first three years with the Mystics.

QUICK STATS

WASHINGTON MYSTICS

Founded: 1998

Championships: 1 (2019)

Key coaches:
- Marianne Stanley (2002–03): 26–40, 3–2 playoffs
- Julie Plank (2009–10): 38–30, 0–4 playoffs
- Mike Thibault (2013–22): 173–155, 14–20 playoffs, 1 WNBA title

Most career points: Alana Beard (3,128)

Most career assists: Natasha Cloud (1,258)

Most career rebounds: Chamique Holdsclaw (1,459)

Most career blocks: Emma Meesseman (193)

Most career steals: Alana Beard (364)

Stats are accurate through the 2024 season.

GLOSSARY

assists
Passes that lead directly to a teammate scoring a basket.

baseline
The line behind the basket on each side of the court.

draft
An event that allows teams to choose new players coming into the league.

fadeaway
A shot taken while moving away from the basket.

pandemic
A disease that spreads quickly around the world.

rally
To come from behind in a game.

rookie
A first-year player.

screen
When an offensive player blocks a defender to create space for a teammate.

upset
An unexpected victory by a supposedly weaker team.

TO LEARN MORE

Graves, Will. *Basketball.* Abdo Publishing, 2024.

O'Neal, Ciara. *The WNBA Finals.* Apex Editions, 2023.

Whiting, Jim, *The Story of the Washington Mystics.* Creative Education, 2024.

MORE INFORMATION

To learn more about the Washington Mystics, go to **pressboxbooks.com/AllAccess**. These links are routinely monitored and updated to provide the most current information available.

INDEX

Beard, Alana, 17–18, 20

Charlotte Sting, 13–14
Chicago Sky, 23, 28
Cloud, Natasha, 8
Connecticut Sun, 18, 24
Curry, Steph, 28

Delle Donne, Elena, 5, 8, 23–26, 28
Durant, Kevin, 28

Edwards, Aaliyah, 27

Harding, Lindsey, 18
Holdsclaw, Chamique, 12–13, 17

Johnson, Sheila C., 15

Langhorne, Crystal, 18, 20
Latta, Ivory, 20

McCray, Nikki, 11–12
Meesseman, Emma, 21, 26

New York Liberty, 5–6, 8, 15

Page, Murriel, 15

Seattle Storm, 24
Smith, Katie, 19
Stewart, Breanna, 5–6
Sykes, Brittany, 6, 8–9, 27

Thibault, Eric, 21
Thibault, Mike, 21